CALIFORNIA
NATIVE AMERICAN TRIBES

LAKE MIWOK
TRIBE

by
Mary Null Boulé

Illustrated by
Daniel Liddell

Merryant Publishers, Inc.
Vashon, WA 98070
206-463-3879

Book Number Thirteen in a series of twenty-six

This series is dedicated to Virginia Harding, whose editing expertise and friendship brought this project to fruition.

Library of Congress Catalog Card Number: 92-61897

ISBN: 1-877599-37-9

Copyright © 1992, Merryant Publishing

7615 S.W. 257th St., Vashon, WA 98070.

FOREWORD

Native American people of the United States are often living their lives away from major cities and away from what we call the mainstream of life. It is, then, interesting to learn of the important part these remote tribal members play in our everyday lives.

More than 60% of our foods come from the ancient Native American's diet. Farming methods of today also can be traced back to how tribal women grew crops of corn and grain. Many of our present day ideas of democracy have been taken from tribal governments. Even some 1,500 Native American words are found in our English language today.

Fur traders bought furs from tribal hunters for small amounts of money, sold them to Europeans and Asians for a great deal of money, and became rich. Using their money to buy land and to build office buildings, some traders started business corporations which are now the base of our country's economy.

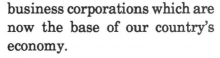

There has never been enough credit given to these early Americans who took such good care of our country when it was still in their care. The time has come to realize tribal contributions to our society today and to give Native Americans not only the credit, but the respect due them.

Mary Boulé

A-frame cradle for girls; tule matting. Tubatulabal tribe.

GENERAL INFORMATION

Creation legends told by today's tribal people speak of how, very long ago, their creator placed them in a territory, where they became caretakers of that land and its animals. None of their ancient legends tells about the first Native Americans coming from another continent.

It is important to respect the different beliefs and theories, to learn from and seek the truth in all of them.

Villagers' tribal history lessons do not agree with the beliefs of anthropologists (scientific historians who study the habits and customs of humans).

Clues found by these scientists lead them to believe that ancient tribespeople came to North America from Asia during the Ice Age period some 20 to 35 thousand years ago. They feel these humans walked over a land strip in the Bering Straits, following animal herds who provided them with food.

Scientists' understanding of ancient people must come from studying clues; for example, tools, utensils, baskets, garbage discoveries, and stories they passed from one generation to the next.

California's Native Americans did not organize into large tribes. Instead they divided into tribelets, sometimes having as many as 250 people. Some tribelets had only one chief for each village.

From 20 to 100 people could be living in one village, which usually had several houses. In most cases, these groups of people were one family and were related to each other. From five to ten people of a family might live in one house. For instance, a mother, a father, two or three children, a grandmother, or aunt or daughter-in-law might live together.

Village members together would own the land important to them for their well-being. Their land might include oak trees with precious acorns, streams and rivers, and plants which were good to eat. Streams and rivers were especially important to a tribe's quality of life. Water drew animals to it; that meant more food for the tribe to eat. Fish were a good source of food, and traveling by boat was often easier than walking long distances. Water was needed in every part of tribal life.

Village and tribelet land was carefully guarded. Each group knew exactly where the boundaries of its land were found. Boundaries were known by landmarks such as mountains or rivers, or they might also be marked by poles planted in the ground. Some boundary lines were marked by rocks, or by objects placed there by tribal members. The size of a territory had to be large enough to supply food to every person living there.

The California tribes spoke many languages. Sometimes villages close together even had a problem understanding one another. This meant that each group had to be sure of the boundaries of other tribes around them when gathering food. It would not be wise to go against the boundaries and the customs of neighbors. The Native Americans found if they respected the boundaries of their neighbors, not so many wars had to be fought. California tribes, in spite of all their differences, were not as warlike as other tribes in our country.

Not only did the California tribes speak different languages, but their members also differed in size. Some tribes were very tall, almost six feet tall. The shortest people came from the Yuki tribe which had territory in what is now Mendocino County. They measured only about 5'2" tall. All Native Americans, regardless of size, had strong, straight black hair and dark brown eyes.

TRADE

Trading between tribes was an important part of life. Inland tribes had large animal hides that coastal tribes wanted. By trading the hides to coastal groups, inland tribes would receive fish and shells, which they in turn wanted. Coastal tribes also wanted minerals and rocks mined in the mountains by inland tribes. Obsidian rock from the northern mountains was especially wanted for arrowheads. There were, as well, several minerals, mined in the inland mountains, which could be made into the colorful body paints needed for religious ceremonies.

Southern tribes particularly wanted steatite from the Gabrielino tribe. Steatite, or soapstone, was a special metal which allowed heat to spread evenly through it. This made it a good choice to be used for cooking pots and flat frying pans. It could be carved into bowls because of its softness and could be decorated by carving designs into it. Steatite came from Catalina Island in the Coastal Gabrielino territory. Gabrielinos found steatite to be a fine trading item to offer for the acorns, deerskins, or obsidian stone they needed.

When people had no items to trade but needed something, they used small strings of shells for money. The small dentalium shells, which came from the far distant Northwest coast, had great value. Strings of dentalia usually served as money in the Northern California tribes, although some dentalia was used in the Central California tribes.

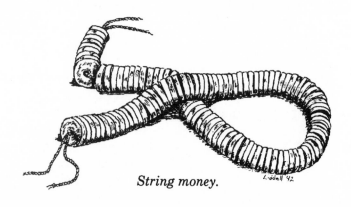

String money.

In southern California clam shells were broken and holes were bored through the center of each piece. Then the pieces were rounded and polished with sandstone and strung into strings for money. These were not thought to be as valuable as dentalia.

Strings of shell money were measured by tattoo marks on the trader's lower arm or hand.

Here is a sample of shell value:

> A house, three strings
> A fishing place, one to three strings
> Land with acorn-bearing oak trees, one to five strings

A great deal of rock and stone was traded among the tribes for making tools. Arrows had to have sharp-edged stone for tips. The best stone for arrow tips was obsidian (volcanic glass) because, when hit properly, it broke off into flakes with very sharp edges. California tribes considered obsidian to be the most valuable rock for trading.

Some tribes had craftsmen who made knives with wooden handles and obsidian blades. Often the handles were decorated with carvings. Such knives were good for trading purposes. Stone mortars and pestles, used by the women for grinding grains into flour, were good trading items.

BASKETS & POTTERY

California tribal women made beautiful baskets. The Pomo and Chumash baskets, what few are left, show us that the women of those tribes might have been some of the finest basketmakers in the world. Baskets were used for gathering and storing food, for carrying babies, and even for hauling water. In emergencies, such as flooding waters, sometimes children, women, and tribal belongings crossed the swollen rivers and streams in huge, woven baskets! Baskets were so tightly woven that not a drop of water could leak from them.

Baskets also made fine cooking pots. Very hot rocks were taken from a fire and tossed around inside baskets with a looped tree branch until food in the basket was cooked.

Most baskets were made to do a certain job, but some baskets were designed for their beauty alone and were excellent for trading. Older women of a tribe would teach young girls how to weave baskets.

Pottery was not used by many California tribes. What little there was seems to have been made by those tribes living near to the Navaho and Mohave tribes of Arizona, and it shows their style. For example, pottery of the California tribes did not have much decoration and was usually a dull red color. Designs were few and always in yellow.

Ohlone hunter wearing deerskin camouflage.

Long thin coils of clay were laid one on top the other. Then the coils were smoothed between a wooden paddle and a small stone to shape the bowl. Pottery from California Native Americans has been described as light weight and brittle (easily broken), probably because of the kind of clay soil found in California.

HUNTING & FISHING

Tribal men spent much of their time making hunting and fishing tools. Bows and arrows were built with great care, to make them shoot as accurately as possible. Carelessly made hunting weapons caused fewer animals to be killed and people then had less food to eat.

Bows made by men of Southern California tribes were made long and narrow. In the northern part of the state bows were a little shorter, thinner, and wider than those of their northern neighbors. Size and thickness of bows depended on the size trees growing in a tribe's territory. The strongest bows were wrapped with sinew, the name given to animal tendons. Sinew is strong and elastic like a rubber band.

Arrows were made in many sizes and shapes, depending on their use. For hunting larger animals, a two-piece arrow was used. The front piece of the arrow shaft was made so that it would remain in the animal, even if the back part was removed or broken off. The arrowhead, or point, was wrapped to the front piece of the shaft. This kind of arrow was also used in wars.

Young boys used a simple wooden arrow with the end sharpened to a point. With this they could hunt small animals like birds and rabbits. The older men of the tribe taught boys how to make their own arrows, how to aim properly, and how to repair broken weapons.

Tribal men spent many hours making and mending fishing nets. The string used in making nets often came from the fibers of plants. These fibers were twisted to make them strong and tough, then knotted into netting. Fences, or weirs, that had one small opening for fish, were built across streams. As the fish swam through the opening they would be caught in netting or harpooned by a waiting fisherman.

Hooks, if used at all, were cut from shells. Mostly hooks could be found when the men fished in large lakes or when catching trout in high mountain areas. Hooks were attached to heavy plant fiber string.

Dip nets, made of netting attached to branches that were bent into a circle, were used to catch fish swimming near shore. Dip nets had long handles so the fishermen could reach deep into the water.

Sometimes a mild poison was placed on the surface of shallow water. This confused the fish and caused them to float to the surface of the water, where they could be scooped up by a waiting fisherman. Not enough poison was used to make humans ill.

Not all fishing was done from the shore. California tribes used two kinds of boats when fishing. Canoes, dug out of one half a log, were useful for river fishing. These were square at each end, round on the bottom, and very heavy. Some of them were well-finished, often even having a carved seat in them.

Today we think of "balsa" as a very lightweight wood, but in Spanish, the word balsa means "raft". That is why Spanish explorers called the Native American canoes, made from tule reeds, "balsa" boats.

Balsa boats were made of bundled tule reeds and were used throughout most of California. They made into safe, light-weight boats for lake and river use. Usually the balsa canoe had a long, tightly tied bundle of tule for the boat bottom and one bundle for each side of the canoe. The front of the canoe was higher than the back. Balsa boats could be steered with a pole or with a paddle, like a raft.

Men did most of the fishing, women were in charge of gathering grasses, seeds, and acorns for food. After the food was collected, it was either eaten right away or made ready for winter storage.

Except for a few southern groups, California tribes had perma-nent villages where they lived most of the year. They also had food-gathering places they returned to each year to collect acorns, salt, fish, and other foods not found near their villages.

FOOD

Many different kinds of plant food grew wild in California in the days before white people arrived. Berries and other plant foods grew in the mountains. Forests offered the local tribes everything from pine nuts to animals.

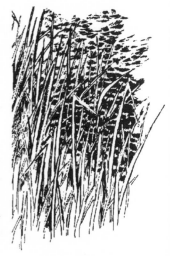

Native Americans found streams full of fish for much of the year. Inland fresh water lakes had large tule reeds growing along their shores. Tule could be eaten as food when plants were young and tender. More important, however, tule was used in making fabric for clothes and for building boats and houses. Tule was probably the most useful plant the California Native Americans found growing wild in their land.

Like all deserts, the one in southern California had little water or fish, but small animals and cactus plants made good food for the local tribes. They moved from place to place harvesting whatever was ripe. Tribal members always knew when and where to find the best food in their territory.

Acorns were the main source of food for all California tribes. Acorn flour was as important to the California Native Americans as wheat is to us today. Five types of California oak trees produced acorns that could be eaten. Those from black oak and tanbark oak seem to have been the favorite kinds.

Since some acorns tasted better than others, the tastiest ones were collected first. If harvest of the favorite acorn was poor some years, then less tasty acorns had to be eaten all winter long.

So important were acorns to California Indians that most tribes built their entire year around them. Acorn harvest marked the beginning of their calendar year. Winter was counted as so many months after acorn harvest, and summer was counted by the number of months before the next acorn harvest.

Acorn harvest ceremonies usually were the biggest events of the year. Most celebrations took place in mid-October and included dancing, feasts, games of chance, and reunions with relatives. Harvest festivals lasted for many days. They were a time of joy for everyone.

The annual acorn gathering lasted two to three weeks. Young boys climbed the oak trees to shake branches; some men used long poles to knock acorns to the ground. Women loaded the nuts into large cone-shaped burden baskets and carried them to a central place where they were put in the sun to dry.

Once the acorns were dried, the women carried them back to the tribe's permanent villages. There they lined special basket-like storage granaries with strong herbs to keep insects away, then stored the acorns inside. Granaries were placed on stilts to keep animals from getting into them and were kept beside tribal houses.

Preparing acorns for each meal was also the women's job. Shells were peeled by hitting the acorns with a stone hammer on an anvil (flat) stone. Meat from the nut was then laid on a stone mortar. A mortar was usually a large stone with a slight dip on its surface. Sometimes the mortar had a bottomless basket, called a hopper, glued to its top. This kept the acorn meat from sliding off the mortar as it was beaten. The meat was then pounded with a long stone pestle. Acorn flour was scraped away from the hopper's sides with a soaproot fiber brush during this process.

From there the flour was put into an open-worked basket and sifted. A fine flour came through the bottom of the basket, while the larger pieces were put back in the mortar for more pounding.

The most important process came after the acorn flour was sifted. Acorn flour has a very bitter-tasting tannin in it. This bitter taste was removed by a method called leaching. Many tribes leached the flour by first scooping out a hollow in sand near water. The hollow was lined with leaves to keep the flour from washing away. A great deal of hot water was poured through the flour to wash out (leach) the bitterness. Sometimes the flour was put into a basket for the leaching process, instead of using sand and leaves.

Finally the acorn flour was ready to be cooked. To make mush, heated stones were placed in the basket with the flour. A looped tree branch or two long sticks were used to toss the hot rocks around so the basket would not burn. When the mush had boiled, it could be eaten. If the flour and water mixture was baked in an earthen oven, it became a kind of bread. Early explorers wrote that it was very tasty.

Historians have estimated that one family would eat from 1500 to 2000 pounds of acorn flour a year. One reason California native Americans did not have to plant seeds and raise crops was because there were so many acorns for them to harvest each year.

Whether they ate fish or shellfish or plant food or animal meat, nature supplied more than enough food for the Native Americans who lived in California long ago. Many believed their good fortune in having fine weather and plenty to eat came from being good to their gods.

RELIGION

Tribal members had strong beliefs in the power of spirits or gods around them. Each tribe was different, but all felt the importance of never making a spirit angry with them. For that reason a celebration to thank the spirit-gods for treating them well, took place before each food gathering and before each hunting trip, and after each food harvest.

Usually spiritual powers were thought to belong to birds or animals. Most California tribespeople felt bears were very wicked and should not be eaten. But Coyote seems to have been a kind leader who helped them if they were in trouble, even though he seems to have been a bit naughty at times. Eagle was thought to be very powerful and good to native Americans. In some tribes, Eagle was almost as powerful as Sun.

Tribes placed importance on different gods, according to the tribe's needs. Rain gods were the most important spirits to desert tribes. Weather gods, who might bring less rain or warmer temperatures, were important to northern tribes. A great many groups felt there were gods for each of the winds: North, South, East and West. The four directions were usually included in their ceremonial dances and were used as part of the decorations on baskets, pots, and even tools.

Animals were not only worshipped and believed to be spirit-gods, like Deer or Antelope, but tribal members felt there was a personal animal guardian for each one of them. If a tribal member had a deer as guardian, then that person could never kill a deer or eat deer meat.

California Native Americans believed in life after death. This made them very respectful of death and very fearful of angering a dead person. Once someone died, the name of the dead person could never again be said aloud. Since it was easy to accidentally say a name aloud, the name was usually given to a new baby. Then the dead person would not become angry.

Shamans were thought to be the keepers of religious beliefs and to have the ability to talk directly to spirit-gods. It was the job of a village shaman to cure sick people, and to speak to the gods about the needs of the people. Some tribes had several kinds of shamans in one village. One shaman did curing, one scared off evil spirits, while another took care of hunters.

Not all shamans were nice, so people greatly feared their power. However, if shamans had no luck curing sick people or did not bring good luck in hunting, the people could kill them. Most shamans were men, but in a few tribes, women were doctors.

Most California tribal myths have been lost to history because they were spoken and never written down. The legends were told and retold on winter nights around the home fires. Sadly, these were forgotten after the missionaries brought Christianity to California and moved tribal members into the missions.

A few stories still remain, however. It is thought by historians that northwest California tribes were the only ones not to have a myth on how they were created. They did not feel that the world was made and prepared for human beings. Instead, their few remaining stories usually tell of mountain peaks or rivers in their own territory.

The central California tribes had creation stories of a great flood where there was only water on earth. They tell of how man was made from a bit of mud that a turtle brought up from the bottom of the water.

Many southwest tribes believed there was a time of no sky or water. They told of two clouds appearing which finally became Sky and Earth.

Throughout California, however, all tribes had myths that told of Eagle as the leader, Coyote as chief assistant, and of less powerful spirits like Falcon or Hawk.

Costumes for religious ceremonies often imitated these animals they worshipped or feared. Much time was spent in making the dance costumes as beautiful as possible. Red woodpecker feathers were so brilliant a color they were used to decorate religious headdresses, necklaces, or belts. Deerskin clothing was fringed so shell beads could be attached to each thin strip of leather.

Eagle feathers were felt to be the most sacred of religious objects. Sometimes they were made into whole robes.

Religious feather charm.

Usually, though, the feathers were used just for decorations. All these costumes were valuable to the people of each tribe. The village chief was in charge of taking care of the costumes, and there was terrible punishment for stealing them. Clothing worn everyday was not fancy like costuming for rituals.

Willow bark skirt.

CLOTHING

Central and southern California's fine weather made regular clothes not really very important to the Native Americans. The children and men went naked most of the year, but most women wore a short apron-like skirt. These skirts were usually made in two pieces, front and back aprons, with fringes cut into the bottom edges. Often the skirt was made from the inner bark of trees, shredded and gathered on a cord. Sometimes the skirt was made from tule or grass.

In northern California and in rainy or windy weather elsewhere in the state, animal-skin blankets were worn by both men and women. They were used like a cape and wrapped around the body. Sometimes the cape was put over one shoulder and under the other arm, then tied in front. All kinds of skins were used; deer, otter, wildcat, but sea-otter fur was thought to be the best. If the skin was from a small animal, it was cut into strips and woven together into a fabric. At night the cape became a blanket to keep the person warm.

Because of the rainy weather in northern California, the women wore basket caps all the time. Women of the central and south tribes wore caps only when carrying heavy loads, where the forehead had to be used as support. Then a cap helped keep too much weight from being placed on the forehead.

Most California people went barefoot in their villages. For journeys into rough land, going to war, wood gathering, or in colder weather, the tribesmen in central and northwest California wore a one-piece soft shoe with no extra sole, which went high up on the leg.

Southern California tribespeople, however, wore sandals most of the time, wearing high, soled moccasins only when they traveled long distances or into the mountains. Leggings of skin were worn in snow, and moccasins were sometimes lined with grass for more comfort and warmth.

VILLAGE LIFE

Houses of the California tribes were made of materials found in their area. Usually they were round with domed roofs. Except for a few tribes, a house floor was dug into the earth a few feet. This was wise, for it made the home warmer in winter and cooler in summer. It also meant that less material was needed to make house walls.

Framework for the walls was made from bendable branches tied to support poles. Some frames of the houses were covered with earth and grass. Others were covered with large slabs of redwood or pine bark. Central California

Split-stick clapper, rhythm instrument. Hupa tribe.

villagers made large woven mats of tule reed to cover the tops and sides of houses. In the warmer southern area, brush and smaller pieces of bark were used for house walls.

Most California Native American villages had a building called a sweathouse, where the men could be found when they were not hunting, fishing or traveling. It was a very important place for the men, who used it rather like a clubhouse. They could sweat and then scrape themselves clean with curved ribs of deer. The sweathouse was smaller than a family house. Normally it had a center pole framework with a firepit on the ground next to the pole. When the fire was lit, some smoke was allowed to escape through a hole at the top of the roof; however, most was trapped inside the building. Smoke and heat were the main reasons for having a sweathouse. Both were believed to be a way to purify tribal members' bodies. Sweathouse walls were mainly hard-packed earth. The heat produced was not a steam heat but came from a wood-fed fire.

In the center of most villages was a large house that often had no walls, just a roof held up with poles. It was here that religious dances and rituals were held, or visitors were entertained.

Dances were enjoyed and were performed with great skill. Music, usually only rhythm instruments, accompanied the dances. For some reason California Native Americans did not use drums to create rhythms for their dances. Three different kinds of rattles were used by California tribes.

One type, split-clap sticks, created rhythm for dancing. These were usually a length of cane (a hollow stick) split in half lengthwise for about two-thirds of its length. The part still uncut was tightly wound with cord so it would not split all the way. The stick was held at the tied end in one hand and hit against the palm of the other hand to make its sound.

19

A pebble-filled moth cocoon made rhythm for shaman duties. These could range from calling on spirits to cure illnesses, to performing dances to bring rain. Probably the best sounds to beat rhythm for songs and dances came from bundles of deer hooves tied together on a stick. These rattles have a hollow, warm sound.

The only really "musical" instrument found in California was a flute made of reed that was played by blowing across the edge of one end. Melodies were not played on any of these instruments. Most North American Indians sang their songs rather than playing melodies on music instruments.

Special songs were sung for each event. There were songs for healing sick people, songs for success in hunting, war, or marriage. Women sang acorn-grinding songs and lullabies. Songs were sung in sorrow for the dead and during story-telling times. Group singing, with a leader, was the favorite kind of singing. Most songs were sung by all tribe members, but religious songs had to be sung by a special group. It was important that sacred songs not be changed through the years. If a mistake was made while singing sacred music, the singer could be punished, so only specially trained singers would sing ritual songs.

All songs were very short, some of them only 20 to 30 seconds long. They were made longer by repeating the melodies over and over, or by connecting several songs together. Songs usually told no story, just repeated words or phrases or syllables in patterns.

Song melodies used only one or two notes and harmony was never added. Perhaps that is why mission Indians, at those missions with musician priests, especially loved to sing harmony in the church choirs.

Songs and dances were good methods of passing rich tribal traditions on to the children. It was important to tribal adults that their children understand and love the tribe's heritage.

Children were truly wanted by parents in most tribes and new parents carefully watched their tiny babies day and night, to be sure they stayed warm and dry. Usually a newborn was strapped into a cradle and tied to the mother's back so she could continue to work, yet be near the baby at all times. In some tribes, older children took care of babies of cradle age during the day to give the mother time to do all her work, while grandmothers were often in charge of caring for toddlers.

Children were taught good behavior, traditions, and tribal rules from babyhood, although some tribes were stricter than others. Most of the time parents made their children obey. Young children could be lightly punished, but in many tribes those over six or seven years old were more severely punished if they did not follow the rules.

Just as children do today, Native American youngsters had childhood traditions they followed. For instance, one tribal tradition said that when a baby tooth came out, a child waited until dusk, faced the setting sun and threw the tooth to the west. There is no mention of a generous tooth fairy, however.

Tribal parents were worried that their offspring might not be strong and brave. Some tribes felt one way to make their children stronger was by forcing them to bathe in ice cold water, even in wintertime. Every once in a while, for example, Modoc children were awakened from sleep and taken to a cold lake or stream for a freezing bath.

But if freezing baths at night were hard on young Native Americans, their days were carefree and happy. Children were allowed to play all day, and some tribes felt children did not even have to come to dinner if they didn't want to. In those tribes, children could come to their houses to eat anytime of the day.

The games boys played are not too different from those played today. Swimming, hide and seek among the tule reeds, a form of tetherball with a mud ball tied to a pole, and willow-javelin throwing kept boys busy throughout the day.

Fathers made their sons small bows and arrows, so boys spent much time trying to improve their hunting skills. They practised shooting at frogs or chipmunks. The first animal any boy killed was not touched or eaten by him. Others would carry the kill home to be cooked and eaten by villagers. This tradition taught boys always to share food.

Another hunting tool for boys was a hollowed-out willow branch. This became like a modern day beanshooter, only the Native American boys shot juniper berries instead of beans. Slingshots made good hunting weapons, as well.

Girls and boys shared many games, but girls playing with each other had contests to see who could make a basket the fastest, or they played with dolls made of tule. Together, young boys and girls played a type of ring-around-the-rosie game, climbed mountains, or built mud houses.

As children grew older, the boys followed their fathers and the girls followed their mothers as the adults did their daily work. Children were not trained in the arts of hunting or basketmaking, however, until they became teenagers.

HISTORY

Spanish missionaries, led by Fray Junipero Serra, arrived in California in 1769 to build missions along the coast of California. By 1823, fifty years later, 21 missions had been founded. Almost all of them were very successful, and the Franciscan monks who ran them were proud of how many Native Americans became Christians.

However, all was not as the monks had planned it would be. Native American people had never been around the diseases European white men brought with them. As a result, they had no immunity to such illnesses as measles, small pox, or flu. Too many mission Indians died from white men's diseases.

Historians figure there were 300,000 Native Americans living in California before the missionaries came. The missions show records of 83,000 mission Indians during mission days. By the time the Mexicans took over the missions from the Spanish in 1834, only 20,000 remained alive.

The great California Gold Rush of 1849 was probably another big reason why many of the Native Americans died during that time. White men, staking their claim to tribal lands with gold upon it, thought nothing of killing any California tribesman who tried to keep and protect his territory. Fifty-thousand tribal members died from diseases, bullets, or starvation between the gold Rush Days and 1870. By 1910, only 17,000 California Indians remained.

Although the American government tried to set aside reservations (areas reserved for Native Americans), the land given to the Indians often was not good land. Worse yet, some of the land sacred to tribes, such as burial grounds, was taken over by white people and never given back.

Sadly, mission Indians, when they became Christians, forgot the proud heritage and beliefs they had followed for thousands of years. Many wonderful myths and songs they had passed from one generation to the next, on winter nights so long ago, have been lost forever.

Today some 100,000 people can claim California Native American ancestors, but few pure-blooded tribespeople remain. Our link with the Wanderers, who came from Asia so long ago, has been forever broken.

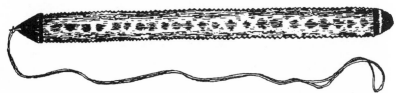

The bullroarer made a deep, loud sound when whirled above the player's head. Tipai tribe.

Villages were usually built beside a lake, stream, or river. Balsa canoes are on the shore. Tule reeds grow along the edge of the water and are drying on poles on the right side of the picture.

Women preparing food in baskets, sit on tule mats. Tule mats are being tied to the willow pole framework of a house being built by one of the men.

LAKE MIWOK TRIBE

INTRODUCTION

The Miwok (Mee' walk) people were divided into three large groups by anthropologists (historians who study the lives of ancient people). They were placed into groups according to the languages they spoke and according to where they lived.

The group named Eastern Miwoks settled inland, on the eastern side of San Francisco Bay. Its territory went from the edge of the bay, east to the Sierra Mountains. Northern-most of the three groups were the Lake Miwoks; and west and south of the Lake Miwoks was the territory of the Coast Miwoks.

The Lake Miwoks were hunters and food gatherers who had most of their permanent villages on creeks in the valleys south of Clear Lake. Even though it was called the Lake Miwok tribe, it had no villages on the edge of the lake itself.

Douglas fir, sugar pine, and yellow pine evergreen trees grew in the higher land of Lake Miwok territory. Live oak trees and chaparral brush were found in the canyons and lower foothills. In the valleys where they lived were oak woodlands.

Territory woodlands provided tribal members with many plants for food, especially oak trees which provided acorns. Pepperwood, laurel, and willow trees grew along streams. Grasses, flowering plants and shrubs like manzanita also grew there.

The oldest village of the Lake Miwok tribe was simply called 'deep place' and was three or four miles south of Lower Lake, a small lake connected to Clear Lake. Many other Lake Miwok villages were found in this area, as well. There was probably no more than a total of 500 Lake Miwok tribal members before white men arrived.

THE VILLAGE

Permanent villages were made up of several kinds of buildings. Tribal houses were round, some of them very large because more than one family lived in them. They were made of materials villagers found in nature around them. Roofs of the homes were conical, like an upside-down ice cream cone.

Poles were used for the framework of a house, with one larger pole in the center to help support the roof and walls. Leaves, brush, and woven tule were piled against the sides of the framework, then dirt was put on top of the brush or tule. The floor of a house was dug several inches into the earth.

One source book says the central doorway always opened to the east, so time could be told by the rising sun. Often a basket was leaned against the door on winter nights, perhaps to keep out the cold winds.

In the summer, however, at food-gathering sites away from their permanent village, the only shelter tribal members needed was a square or circle of willow sticks tied together with wild grapevines and covered with grass or brush.

Every permanent village had a large round ceremonial building, bigger than any house, where dances and religious rituals took place. Some of these ceremonial houses were

Miwok roundhouse.

27

from forty to fifty feet across at floor level, with the floor dug into the ground three to four feet. Thatch, or brush, and dirt were firmly packed around the bottom edges of the walls so water would not pour into the building when it rained. A ceremonial house was entered by way of several long tunnels.

A sweathouse was found in every village. It was a small building that looked like a dirt mound, where men of the village spent their time when they were not hunting or fishing. Fishing nets were mended there, as were bows and arrows.

The main purpose of a sweathouse, however, was to keep men's bodies purified by causing them to sweat. Heat in the sweathouse came from large fires placed in the center of the small building. Men would test each other to see who could stand the hottest temperature. When a man could stand the heat no longer, he would rush outside and plunge himself into a nearby stream of cold water.

A man who was called a sweathouse keeper was in charge of a sweathouse. Among his duties was a ritual in which he asked the spirits to keep a newborn baby strong.

VILLAGE LIFE

When a baby was born, the new mother was placed in a special hut for the birth. She stayed there until the baby was a few weeks old. A baby was often named for a long-dead relative. A string-bead necklace was placed around the baby's neck when it was named.

An orphaned child was often adopted by another person but people were not allowed to adopt a child unless they had a dream telling them to do so. Bead necklaces were placed around the children's necks at the time of adoption to show they had officially become relatives of the person who adopted them.

*Only when a young man could
hunt was he considered old enough to marry.*

There seems to have been teenage ceremonies for both boys and girls, but there is little information about what happened at the ceremonies. It is known that both boys and girls fasted (went without certain foods for a period of time) during their ceremonies. Both boys and girls could only eat turtle meat and fish while the ceremony lasted. Plant foods could be eaten by all the teenagers during this time, however, so they did not go hungry.

It was during this early teenage period that the boys were finally given permission to hunt with the adult tribal hunters. Only when a young man could hunt was he considered old enough to marry, for he had to be capable of supporting a family with his own hunting abilities.

Marriage in the Lake Miwok tribe seems to have been arranged by parents. A marriage was the time for an exchange of gifts between the families of the bride and groom. Beads, baskets, and other such presents were thought to be proper gifts at this time.

Although little information has been found about the raising of Lake Miwok children, like most California tribes their training was probably left to the grandparents. Grandparents had more time to do the training because they were no longer required to spend their days finding food and preparing or preserving it.

When a villager died, there were special rituals which had to be performed. A time was always set aside for mourning. During the mourning period, adults were allowed to cry, something they were not to do at any other time.

Bodies were either buried or cremated. If a body was cremated, the dead person's belongings were also thrown into the cremation fire. If a body was buried, the belongings were buried with the body.

Close relatives of a person who died cut their hair short for the mourning period. Men relatives did not go to the sweathouse for several days after a funeral. The widow of a man who died singed (burned the ends of) her hair and put a mixture of white clay and pine tree pitch on the burned ends.

If the tribal member who died was an important person, a second cremation fire was burned a year later. At that time, any remains of the important villager were burned again. New offerings of baskets or other gifts were thrown into the fire in memory of the dead person.

Sometimes a village shaman dreamed that certain dead people needed food and clothing. The shaman would claim he had been told this by the dead, themselves. When this happened, a long pole was placed upright in the ground. An image of the dead person or persons, possibly made from a deerskin blanket, was attached to the top of the pole. Sometimes valuable beads were put inside the image.

Gifts of food were piled at the bottom of the pole while villagers danced around it. A village shaman talked and said prayers in memory of the dead person, then gifts and the pole were burned. This image ceremony was not only to send needed gifts to a dead villager but also was a way of remembering the one who had died.

The leader of a village was called a chief. Although most chiefs were men, inheriting their jobs from their fathers, women sometimes held the title of chief. A woman might be chief if she were the wife of a former leader, and they had no sons. It was the duty of a chief to give speeches to tribal members, explaining how they should behave and how they should do their jobs. Proper behavior was important to tribal members. For instance, no villager was allowed to spit in a public place. It was the job of a chief to remind people of the village rule on spitting.

Another Lake Miwok rule concerned tribal members' names. Villagers were suspicious of a stranger who came to their village and asked the name of a villager. Names were considered private property and tribal members thought it rude of anyone, stranger or not, to ask the name of a Miwok person.

A chief was helped by an assistant, who carried out the leader's orders. There were also specially trained people who handled dances, feasts, and religious ceremonies. Each village had a woman, often the chief's wife, who was in charge of all village women.

RELIGION

Shamans were the religious and ceremonial leaders of the villages, as well as curing doctors. Their jobs as curing doctors probably kept them the busiest. There were two kinds of curing doctors: those whose jobs were to physically remove a disease from a sick villager, and those who used their spirit powers, or their singing, to cure someone.

The shamans who claimed they could actually remove a disease from the body were much like our magicians today. They used sleight-of-hand tricks which made it look as though feathers, stones, obsidian flakes and other objects were coming from the sick person's body. These objects were supposed to be symbols of the disease. This kind of shaman would even cut the skin of the sick person and draw blood in the hope of removing a disease.

The second kind of curing doctor used only dancing and singing to cure an illness. This kind of shaman claimed to have a direct route to the spirit-gods, who would then cure the sick person. Dancing and singing shamans worked very hard at curing. They went without food, sometimes four days and nights in a row, and slept little during the doctoring of a patient. Sometimes the shaman became sick, and his wife or assistant had to take over. This kind of doctor was thought to have the most spirit power.

When singing was not enough to bring good health back to villagers, herbs and other objects were used in curing. A poultice (something to draw infection out of the body) of shaved tree bark was often put on sore spots. Splints for broken bones were made from the inside wood of elderberry trees.

Large leaves from a plant called the "stinging bush" were placed over a broken bone to help it heal. Pepperwood leaves were held to the cheek for relief from an aching tooth. Bear meat was supposed to be good for treating a cold. Some springs of fresh water were thought to have a special power to cure people. Many of the herbs and plants used by the curing doctors are still used today by modern doctors for the curing of pain.

Shamans were usually trained by older shamans. The medicines used and the songs which were sung often came from a young shaman's father or grandfather. Young shamans in training seemed to come from the families of older shamans. Perhaps the position was an inherited one.

Curing songs were considered to be a shaman's own property and could not be sung by others without permission. A shaman did not ask payment for curing someone, cured people paid what they thought the treatment was worth.

There was also a secret society of doctors known as bear shamans. In order to become a member of this society, persons had to prove themselves powerful. To join the Bear shamans' society, a person had to stop a large rock as it rolled down a hill. Many strange and imaginary

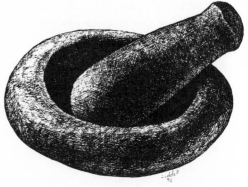

Mortar and pestles were used by the shaman to make medicines.

tales were told about bear shamans. They were supposed to be able to travel great distances at superhuman speed. Women bear shamans were thought to use their powers to gather food and sea shells from faraway places.

Stories were told about how the men were especially dangerous and might kill others. Bear shaman men and women wore bear skins and the men also wore a breastplate of armor. These shamans were greatly feared by villagers.

Lake Miwok religion was built from a rich backlog of myths. Tribal tales told of an ancient past when beings were a combination of humans and animals. These beliefs led to stories of Old Man Coyote, who had both good and bad human behavior. Lake Miwoks thought Coyote had formed the world and made its people out of wood. This was one of the good things Old Man Coyote did. But people could never be sure of Coyote; he was just human enough to be bad as often as he was good. Besides stories of Coyote, Sun and Moon were mentioned in tribal myths and were believed to be powerful gods.

Lake Miwok people felt both plants and animals had power over them. Villagers believed someone could suffer from sore feet if that person imitated a meadowlark's call. It was felt that bothering a porcupine might cause a headache or a nose bleed. Lizards with forked tails were supposed to bring good luck but saving the rattles from a rattlesnake brought bad luck. Keeping a quail as a pet was also thought to be bad luck. Adult tribal members always prayed to a new moon for good health.

All animals killed for food were believed to be under the control of spirit-gods and did not actually die when they were killed, but lived on in spirit.

Religious ceremonies took place in the large dance house built for that purpose. Women did not go into the building except for special occasions. Among those special events were ritual dances. Many dances, like the Big Head Dance,

Big Head dancer.

lasted for four days and nights. Such dances had to be performed exactly the same way each time, so a person was put in charge to make sure there were no performing mistakes. That tribal member was known as the dance caretaker and was a very important villager.

The caretaker, dancers, and all others included in a dance had to fast during the dancing ceremonies. Special costumes were worn. In the case of The Big Head Dance, all dancers wore feather headdresses, and the most important dancer wore the Big Head feather headband.

Other dances celebrated through the year were the Coyote Dance, held when someone had recovered from a sickness; First Fruits Ceremony, held in the spring when flowers bloomed, and the Old Time Dance in which all adults took part.

There were no tribal instruments that played a melody, but whistles were sometimes blown. Singers sang to accompany the dancers. Rhythm for dances was made with rattles and splitsticks. Rattles were made from elderberry branches, hollowed-out fir cones with pebbles placed inside, or from the cocoons of caterpillars. Most instruments were decorated with hawk, blue jay, or robin feathers.

CLOTHING

Feathers and beads were also worn to decorate what little everyday clothing was worn. Even though children seldom wore clothing, holes were made in their ears with a sharp stick or bone so they could wear shell earrings. If men wore clothing, it was usually a deerskin breechcloth. Women wore a skirt at all times and used shell beads as ornaments.

Both men and women wore their hair in braids, and men often wore hairnets of vegetable fiber. Hair was cut with an obsidian (volcanic glass) flake and combed with any stiff plant stem.

When the weather became cool, tribal members wore blankets made of woven rabbit fur strips. Sometimes woodrat fur strips were intertwined with the rabbit strips to form a design. Deerskins were made into blankets. The blanket-capes became just blankets at bedtime.

Ordinarily, tribal members went barefooted but for long trips, cold weather, or in times of war, knee-high moccasins were worn. The California style of moccasin was usually made of one piece of soft deerskin, with a seam up the front and up the back of the heel. The legging part of the moccasin came up to about as high as modern knee socks do today.

Dyes used for coloring clothing or bodies came from plants growing around the villages. Green oak tree galls (swellings on a tree caused by fungus or insects) were squeezed to get permanent blue-black ink . This dye was used for tattooing the body, as well. Burned pepperwood berries were used to mark the skin for dance ceremonies. Boiled tan oak bark made a good dye for hair nets.

BASKETS

Miwok baskets were especially well-made. They were needed in every part of tribal life and used for cooking, carrying, and for storage. Many of the baskets were beautiful as well as practical; women often made them just for artistic reasons.

Willow branches were used for the coiled baskets; coils made of three and four sticks could be so tightly woven that baskets made in this manner could carry water without leaking. Grass roots, gathered each autumn, and fresh pine tree roots bound the coils together. To make the color designs, bullrush roots were blackened in ashes and woven into the coils. Red bud sprouts were used to make red color designs.

Lake Miwok men were some of the few California tribal men who made baskets. They often wove the bell-shaped carrying baskets and made the netting sacks they needed to carry their belongings.

Special baskets were woven to hold babies. Some of them were made to fit on the mother's back. Others were cradles that lay flat for babies to sleep on. Mothers always kept their babies close to them while they worked.

Ceremonial baskets were made to be as beautiful as possible. They were decorated with bits of abalone shells and bright bird feathers, woven into the baskets in lovely designs. Baskets with these kinds of decorations were stored in dry pepperwood leaves to keep moths from eating the feathers.

Twined winnowing baskets were round and almost flat. Their purpose was to help the women remove the outer cover of grain they had gathered. By throwing the grain into

Netting sack.

the air, wind would blow away the cover, and the heavier grain would fall back into the tray. Seed-beater baskets helped the women collect seeds more easily. Loosely woven baskets acted as strainers.

When the bottom of a smaller basket wore out, the remaining part of the basket was glued to the top of a flat stone mortar with tar. This was called a hopper basket and was used when a woman was pounding grains or acorns, to keep the bits of food from falling off the mortar.

FOOD

The gathering of food was a full time job for tribal women, while hunting took much of the men's time. Women did all of the plant, nut, and seed gathering, as well as some fishing; the men were in charge of hunting for animals and fishing for larger fish.

Villagers ate greens during the summer when plants were leafy and full. They also ate wild berries and fruits growing around them in the warm months. Nuts, roots, and preserved meat and fish kept them alive in winter months.

Eastern Miwok granary.

By far the most important food to the California Native Americans was the nut of oak trees, the acorn. Each fall the villagers went long distances to oak groves to collect enough acorns for the winter. Several kinds were gathered and stored in village granaries. Later the acorns were pounded, leached, and made into a flour which was used to make soups, mush, and bread.

Acorn cakes were made by mixing valley oak flour with red soil called "Indian baking powder," which helped take away the bitter taste of the acorn. The cakes were cooked by wrapping them in nests of black oak leaves, putting them between layers of hot rocks, covering them with dirt, and leaving them to bake overnight. The cooked cakes were completely black when done and very sweet tasting.

The Lake Miwok people also ate nuts of both the yellow and sugar pine trees. They enjoyed roasting and eating the nuts from still-green pine cones. Pitch from pine trees made good chewing gum. Manzanita berries were pounded into flour that was later dampened, rolled into balls, and eaten as candy.

Salt came from deposits found in the mountains and along creeks. Other spices, used to make food more tasty, came from many of the same plants we use today.

The most important meat eaten by the tribe was deer meat. So important was deer meat to them that the word in Lake Miwok language which stood for meat was actually their word for "deer." Tribal men hunted deer all year long. Hunters either trapped deer in snares along game trails or chased deer until the animals became worn out and could be easily killed with a bow and arrow. The meat was eaten fresh or salted and dried for jerky.

Nothing of a deer was wasted; bones were saved, warmed, and cracked open so the marrow could be eaten. Deer blood was mixed with ground rabbit bones in watertight baskets, allowed to clot, then baked between leaves in the hot coals of a fire. This looked rather like crumbly cottage cheese and had good flavor.

Grizzly bears and elk were hunted for their meat. Smaller animals, such as rabbits, quail, and woodpeckers were trapped in snares and nets. Yellowjacket eggs were carefully collected and roasted, as were grasshoppers. Both foods were considered tasty favorites of the tribe.

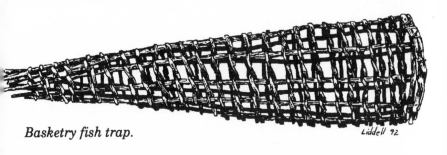

Basketry fish trap.

Liddell '92

Fish were caught in streams by weirs, basketry traps, and nets. Weirs were fences built across a stream of water with only one small opening in them. At the opening, fishermen had either placed a trap or stood ready to spear a fish as it tried to go through the opening. Nets were made from vegetable fiber the men twisted together. Twisting one or two fibers together made a strong cord, that could be knotted into netting.

In slow-moving streams, fishermen spread a mild poison over the surface of the water. This confused the fish, causing them to float to the top of the water, where the men could spear them. Fish was eaten fresh or preserved by either drying it in the sun on wooden frames or by baking it.

Obsidian knife blade.

TOOLS AND WEAPONS

California Native Americans found many uses for stone. Flat large rocks became mortars for the women to pound on when grinding grain and seed with a pestle. Obsidian, a volcanic glass, flaked into pieces with sharp edges. It, and less strong flint, were used for knives, axes, tips of spears, and arrowheads. Deer antlers made fine flaking tools for chipping the obsidian and flint.

Bows were made from hazelwood, oak, or dogwood branches. Lake Miwok hunters also traded for the fine sinew-backed bows made by the Pomo Tribe to the north of them. Elder or willow branches were used to make good arrows. A hunter's extra arrows were carried in a quiver made from the skin of a wildcat or from bear-cub fur. Arrowheads were often poisoned with powder made from drying and pounding the red sacs of black widow spiders.

GAMES

Although villagers worked hard every day, they did take time to have fun. Outside games were played on flat pieces of land. One favorite field game of the Lake Miwoks was a game called handball. It used a ball made of rolled-up angelica leaves, tightly tied with vegetable fiber cord. Players stood in a circle and batted the ball back and forth with their hands. When players missed catching the ball, they were out of the game. The game continued until only one player was left.

Women liked to play a dice game called *múlli*. Dice were made by cutting branches in half and then into smaller sections. Designs were burned into the smooth sides of each section. The dice were about four inches across and eight or nine inches long. Two teams, of as many people as wanted to play, would take turns throwing the dice trying to make them land design side up. Points were given for the number of dice landing with the design showing. Whichever team earned the most points won.

Tribal men also liked games of chance. One of these, called the grass game, was on the order of our game, "Button,

button; who's got the button?" In their game, however, willow sticks or rabbit bones were used instead of buttons. "Hoop and pole", "Shinney", and "Cat's Cradle" also were played by the tribe,

TRADE

The Lake Miwok traders went great distances to trade, traveling as far west as Bodega Bay. Although little is known about what products they wanted or what they used in trade, it is known that they manufactured magnesite cylinders. These cylinders were much desired by other tribes and so had great value. The tribal men also made olivella shell beads, useful as decorations rather than money, which made excellent trading products.

If what they had to offer for trade was not valuable enough for what they wanted, however, then shell money was used. This was money made by the Lake Miwoks in the form of clamshell disk beads.

To figure the value of shell money, the polished beads were strung together on vegetable fiber cord that was of an exact length. Traders tattooed marks on their arms in order to measure the length of a money string accurately. The value of a string of disks depended on the color of the bead, how alike the shell beads were, and how even in size the beads were.

Lake Miwok traders manufactured magnesite cylinders which were much desired by other tribes and so had great value. The tribal men also made olivella shell beads, but they were used for ornaments rather than for money.

HISTORY

Lake Miwok people became mission Indians at the San Rafael, San Francisco Solano, and San José Missions. When Mexico took over the missions from Spain in 1834, the land promised to the Indians by Spain was not given to them. Instead, Mexican officers took the land for themselves, offering the mission Indians jobs working in the fields or hiring them as house servants.

One Mexican landowner decided a Lake Miwok tribal member had killed one of his cows. He took a large group of white men to one of the tribe's villages and killed many Lake Miwoks, as well as taking several hundreds of them back to his ranch as prisoners to work in his fields.

In 1840, the brother of the rancher, a Mexican general named Vallejo, signed a peace treaty with several of the Lake Miwok chiefs. Shortly after this, California became a state and American white settlers began to settle on Lake Miwok land.

Unfortunately, two American settlers were so cruel to tribal members that both Americans were finally killed by the Lake Miwoks. In revenge for the death of the settlers, United States Army troops raided the Lake Miwok tribe, killing a large number of them.

Tribal members were not only killed by warfare with white people, they also died from white people's diseases. Measles and smallpox killed Native Americans by the thousands. Before the arrival of the Spanish missionaries, there were about 500 people in the Lake Miwok tribe. In 1905, only 41 tribal members were counted in a United States census. In 1975, the only remaining settlement of Lake Miwoks was at a place called the Middletown rancheria where a few older tribal members lived at that time.

LAKE MIWOK TRIBE OUTLINE

I. Introduction
    A. Three groups of people
    B. Territory
    C. Trees and plants in territory
    D. Oldest village

II. The village
    A. Four kinds of houses
    B. Assembly house
    C. Sweathouse

III. Village Life
    A. Newborn babies
    B. Orphan children
    C. Teenage ceremonies
    D. Marriage
    E. Training of children
    F. Death customs and rituals
    G. The chief

IV. Religion
    A. Shamans
        1. Kinds of curing and herbal medicine
        2. Training of shamans
        3. Bear shamans
    B. Myths
    C. Ceremonies
        1. Dances
        2. Rhythm instruments

V. Clothing
    A. Everyday clothing

X. Trade

    A. Distance traveled

    B. Products traded

XI. History

    A. Missions

    B. Mexican takeover

    C. American settlers

    D. Tribe today

GLOSSARY

AWL: a sharp, pointed tool used for making small holes in leather or wood

CEREMONY: a meeting of people to perform formal rituals for a special reason; like an awards ceremony to hand out trophies to those who earned honors

CHERT: rock which can be chipped off, or flaked, into pieces with sharp edges

COILED: a way of weaving baskets which looks like the basket is made of rope coils woven together

DIAMETER: the length of a straight line through the center of a circle

DOWN: soft, fluffy feathers

DROUGHT: a long period of time without water

DWELLING: a building where people live

FLETCHING: attaching feathers to the back end of an arrow to make the arrow travel in a straight line

GILL NET: a flat net hanging vertically in water to catch fish by their heads and gills

GRANARIES: basket-type storehouses for grains and nuts

HERITAGE: something passed down to people from their long-ago relatives

LEACHING: washing away a bitter taste by pouring water through foods like acorn meal

MORTAR: flat surface of wood or stone used for the grinding of grains or herbs with a pestle

PARCHING: to toast or shrivel with dry heat

PESTLE: a small stone club used to mash, pound, or grind in a mortar

PINOLE: flour made from ground corn

INDIAN RESERVATION: land set aside for Native Americans by the United States government

RITUAL: a ceremony that is always performed the same way

SEINE NET: a net which hangs vertically in the water, encircling and trapping fish when it is pulled together

SHAMAN: tribal religious men or women who use magic to cure illness and speak to spirit-gods

SINEW: stretchy animal tendons

STEATITE: a soft stone (soapstone) mined on Catalina Island by the Gabrielino tribe; used for cooking pots and bowls

TABOO: something a person is forbidden to do

TERRITORY: land owned by someone or by a group of people

TRADITION: the handing down of customs, rituals, and belief, by word of mouth or example, from generation to generation

TREE PITCH: a sticky substance found on evergreen tree bark

TWINING: a method of weaving baskets by twisting fibers, rather than coiling them around a support fiber

NATIVE AMERICAN WORDS
WE KNOW AND USE

PLANTS AND TREES
hickory
pecan
yucca
mesquite
saguaro

ANIMALS
caribou
chipmunk
cougar
jaguar
opossum
moose

STATES
Dakota – friend
Ohio – good river
Minnesota – waters that
    reflect the sky
Oregon – beautiful water
Nebraska – flat water
Arizona
Texas

FOODS
avocado
hominy
maize (corn)
persimmon
tapioca
succotash

GEOGRAPHY
bayou – marshy body of
    water
savannah – grassy plain
pasadena – valley

WEATHER
blizzard
Chinook (warm, dry wind)

FURNITURE
hammock

HOUSE
wigwam
wickiup
tepee
igloo

INVENTIONS
toboggan

BOATS
canoe
kayak

OTHER WORDS
caucus – group meeting
mugwump – loner politician
squaw – woman
papoose – baby

CLOTHING
moccasin
parka
mukluk – slipper
poncho

BIBLIOGRAPHY

Cressman, L. S. *Prehistory of the Far West.* Salt Lake City, Utah: University of Utah Press, 1977.

Geiger, Maynard, O.F.M., Ph.D. *The Indians of Mission Santa Barbara.* Santa Barbara, CA 93105: Franciscan Fathers, 1986.

Heizer, Robert F., volume editor. *Handbook of North American Indians; California, volume 8.* Washington, D.C.: Smithsonian Institute, 1978.

Heizer, Robert F. and Elsasser, Albert B. *The Natural World of the California Indians.* Berkeley and Los Angeles, CA; London, England: University of California Press, 1980.

Heizer, Robert F. and Whipple, M.A.. *The California Indians.* Berkeley and Los Angeles, CA; London, England: University of California Press, 1971.

Heuser, Iva. *California Indians.* PO Box 352, Camino, CA 95709: Sierra Media Systems, 1977.

Macfarlen, Allen and Paulette. *Handbook of American Indian Games.* 31 E. 2nd Street, Mineola, N.Y. 11501: Dover Publications, 1985.

Murphey, Edith Van Allen. *Indian Uses of Native Plants.* 603 W. Perkins Street, Ukiah, CA 95482: Mendocino County Historical Society, © renewal, 1987.

National Geographic Society. *The World of American Indians.* Washington, DC: National Geographic Society reprint, 1989.

Tunis, Edwin. *Indians.* 2231 West 110th Street, Cleveland, OH: The World Publishing Company, 1959.

Credits:
Island Industries, Vashon Island, Washington 98070
Dona McAdam, Mac on the Hill, Seattle, Washington 98109

Acknowledgements:
Richard Buchen, Research Librarian, Braun Library,
Southwest Museum
Special thanks